ENCYCLOPÆDIA
Britannica®

Dinosaurs

Publications International, Ltd.

Get the App!

This book is enhanced by an app that can be downloaded from the App Store or Google Play*. Apps are available to download at no cost. Once you've downloaded the app to your smartphone**, use the QR code found on page 3 of this book to access an immersive, 360° virtual reality environment. Then slide the phone into the VR viewer and you're ready to go.

Compatible Operating Systems

- Android 4.1 (JellyBean) or later

- iOS 8.0 or later

Compatible Phones

Removing your device from its case may provide a better fit in the viewer. If your smartphone meets the above operating system requirements and has gyroscope functionality it should support GoogleVR. Publications International, Ltd. has developed and tested this software with the following devices:

- Google Nexus 5, Google Nexus 5X, Google Nexus 6P, Google Pixel

- Apple iPhone 6, Apple iPhone 6S, Apple iPhone 6 Plus, Apple iPhone 6S Plus, Apple iPhone 7, Apple iPhone 7 Plus

- Samsung Galaxy S5, Samsung Galaxy S5 Active, Samsung Galaxy S5 Sport, Samsung Galaxy S6, Samsung Galaxy S6 edge, Samsung Galaxy S6 edge +, Samsung Galaxy Note 4, Samsung Galaxy Note edge, Samsung Galaxy S7, Samsung Galaxy S7 edge, Samsung Galaxy Note 5, Samsung Galaxy S8

Caution

The viewer should not be exposed to moisture or extreme temperatures. The viewer is not water resistant. It is potentially combustible if the lenses are left facing a strong light source.

Cover art from Shutterstock.com

Interior art from Encyclopædia Britannica, Inc., National Park Service, and Shutterstock.com

App content from Encyclopædia Britannica, Inc., Filament Games, Library of Congress, and Shutterstock.com

 Publications International, Ltd.

For inquiries email: customer_service@pubint.com

ISBN: 978-1-64030-166-5

Manufactured in China.

8 7 6 5 4 3 2 1

*We reserve the right to terminate the apps.
**Smartphone not included. Standard data rates may apply to download. Once downloaded, the app does not use data or require wifi access.

DINOSAURS

INSTRUCTIONS

1 Carefully remove the viewer from the book along the perforated edge. Gently push each side of the viewer inward. Then push the front of the viewer into place.

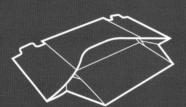 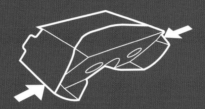 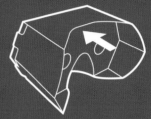

2 Download PI VR Dinosaurs, available on the App Store or Google Play. Direct links to the store locations are found at: pilbooks.com/PIVRDinosaurs.

3 Launch the app. If you are asked to calibrate the viewer, go to page 64 and follow the instructions found there. If asked, allow the app to take photos/videos.

4 When the app loads, you will be prompted to scan the QR code found to the right to verify your possession of this book.

5 You will see a double image of a dinosaur dig on your phone. Slide your smartphone into the front compartment of the VR viewer. The line between the two images should line up with the seam found on the bottom of the viewer, between the two lenses. If your screen seems blurry, make sure the smartphone is aligned precisely with the center of the viewer. Adjusting the phone left or right a few millimeters can make a big difference. The tilt of the viewer and the phone can also affect how the screen looks to you.

6 Look around to explore! PI VR Dinosaurs does not require a lever or remote control. You control each interaction with your gaze. When you see a loading circle, keep your gaze focused until it loads fully to access videos, slideshows, and games.

Loading

7 Gaze at the X to close out of video, slideshow, or game screens.

Exit

CONTENTS

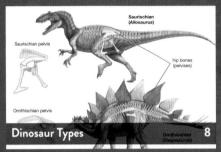
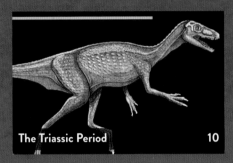

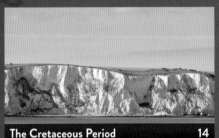

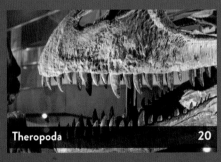

INTRODUCTION

The reptiles known as dinosaurs were the dominant land animals on Earth during most of the Mesozoic Era (252 to 66 million years ago). They thrived for nearly 180 million years. Dinosaurs were diverse animals, with widely varying lifestyles and adaptations. They included meat eaters and plant eaters, animals who walked on two legs and on four, and animals with a solitary lifestyle and those who lived in a herd. Fossil evidence shows that dinosaurs ranged in size from smaller than a chicken to more than 10 times larger than the largest elephant. From studying dinosaur remains, scientists have concluded that dinosaurs were the ancient relatives of today's crocodiles, snakes, lizards, and birds.

FIVE FAST FACTS

1. The remains or traces of dinosaurs were first discovered in the early 19th century.

2. Dinosaur fossils have been found on every continent, including Antarctica.

3. At least 1,000 species of dinosaur have been identified.

4. Scientists classify dinosaurs within a larger group of animals called archosaurs. This group includes modern-day crocodilians (crocodiles, alligators, and their relatives) and birds, as well as the extinct pterosaurs (flying reptiles, such as *Pterodactylus*).

5. Also included in the archosaurs are the extinct predatory reptiles formerly called thecodonts. The latter were among the earliest archosaurs, and some scientists believe that the first dinosaurs were descended from this group.

JURASSIC PERIOD
145 million years ago

The continents shifted during the Mesozoic Era.

THE WORLD OF THE DINOSAURS

When dinosaurs first evolved, the Earth was very different from what it is today. All of the land on Earth formed one gigantic supercontinent, called Pangea (Pangaea). Over millions of years, the supercontinent broke up into separate landmasses that gradually resembled today's continents. Dinosaurs lived throughout this ancient world, in habitats ranging from tropical forests to dry, sandy deserts. During the Mesozoic era the Earth was warmer than it is today. There were no polar ice caps, but there were several seasons in temperate regions. The world was a complex place with many different ecosystems and ecological communities. Dinosaur species living in these ecosystems had to adapt to the climate and environment of their surroundings. Such circumstances allowed the dinosaurs to evolve into a highly diverse group.

Most scientists believe that all dinosaurs reproduced by laying eggs. Infant dinosaurs grew very quickly, in some cases increasing some 16,000 times in size before reaching adulthood.

Some scientists believe that dinosaurs were gray or green in color. These colors would have helped the dinosaurs blend in with their surroundings. Other scientists think that dinosaurs were very colorful. Bright colors would have helped males get the attention of females.

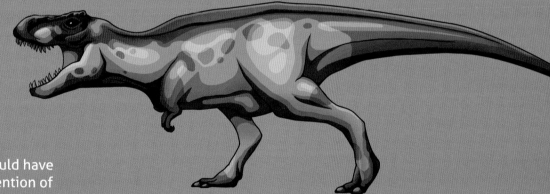

USE THE VR VIEWER AND ASSOCIATED APP

Enhance your experience by using the app! Put your smartphone in the VR viewer and you'll be able to find out more about North American dinosaurs and dinosaur digs!

DINOSAUR TYPES

All dinosaurs divided among two major orders: the Saurischia (lizard-hipped) and the Ornithischia (bird-hipped). Scientists classify dinosaur species into these orders based on their pelvic, or hip, structures. However, the terms saurischian and ornithischian are based on skeletal features and do not indicate evolutionary relationships: in fact, the dinosaurs that gave rise to birds were saurischians; and neither group was closely related to the lizards of the time.

SAURISCHIA

The Saurischia were a particularly diverse group; the order includes both carnivorous and herbivorous dinosaurs who looked, behaved, moved, and foraged in very different ways.

Within the order Saurischia are two major subgroups—the theropods and the sauropodomorphs, the subgroup that includes the sauropods and prosauropods. The theropods were bipedal, meaning that they walked or ran on their two hindlimbs. They also were carnivorous, or meat-eating, predators that hunted prey. Among the best-known theropods are *Velociraptor*, *Allosaurus*, and *Tyrannosaurus rex*. Modern birds are closely related to this group, because they share a common ancestor from the late Jurassic period about 150 million years ago.

Most of the sauropodomorphs were quadrupedal, meaning that they stood and walked on all four limbs; however, some of their earliest members were small and bipedal. The sauropodomorphs were herbivorous, or plant-eating, dinosaurs that browsed the lush vegetation present during the Mesozoic era.

- Saurischia
  - Sauropodomorpha
    - Prosauropoda
    - Sauropoda
  - Theropoda
    - Ceratosauria
    - Tetanurae
- Ornithischia
  - Cerapoda
    - Ornithopoda
    - Pachycephalosauria
    - Ceratopsia
  - Thyreophora
    - Stegosauria
    - Ankylosauria

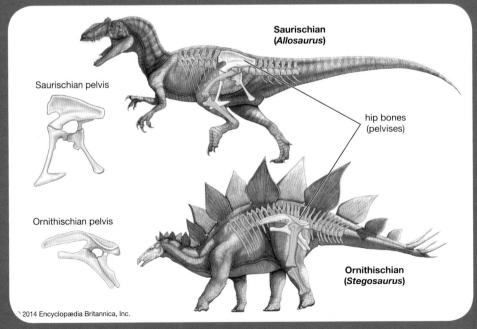

Saurischian (*Allosaurus*)

Saurischian pelvis

hip bones (pelvises)

Ornithischian pelvis

Ornithischian (*Stegosaurus*)

© 2014 Encyclopædia Britannica, Inc.

Baryonyx, a theropod, was a large, carnivorous, probably fish-eating dinosaur that inhabited England during the early Cretaceous period, about 98 to 144 million years ago.

ORNITHISCIA

All members of the order Ornithischia were herbivores, or plant eaters, who had several unique characteristics that adapted them to browsing the lush vegetation present during the Mesozoic era. One such feature was the presence of a central bone, called the predentary, at the tip of the lower jaw. Most species had a toothless, horn-covered beak used to nip off vegetation. Also present were leaf-shaped cheek teeth, which were well adapted for grinding plant material. Yet another unique characteristic was muscular cheek pouches. These cheek pouches stored plant matter in the dinosaurs' mouths and prevented it from falling out as they chewed.

Dinosaurs within the order Ornithischia are further classified into different subgroups, though these categories change frequently as paleontologists rethink classification schemes. Among the major groups are the duck-billed dinosaurs, such as *Iguanodon* and *Maiasaura*; the great horned dinosaurs, such as *Triceratops*; and the dome-headed dinosaurs, such as *Pachycephalosaurus*. Other well-known ornithischians include the armored dinosaurs, such as *Ankylosaurus*, and the plated dinosaurs, such as *Stegosaurus*.

Diplodocus, a sauropod, was an enormous herbivorous dinosaur that inhabited North America during the late Jurassic period.

THE TRIASSIC PERIOD

The Mesozoic ("middle life") era lasted from 252 million to about 66 million years ago. It is divided into three periods: the Triassic (252 million to 201 million years ago), the Jurassic (201 million to 145 million years ago), and the Cretaceous (145 to 66 million years ago).

THE EARLIEST DINOSAURS

The oldest known dinosaurs lived during the Triassic period. Among the oldest species known from this period were *Eodromaeus*, *Eoraptor*, and *Herrerasaurus*. All three were relatively small animals and lived in what is now South America. *Eodromaeus* and *Herrerasaurus* were carnivores, or meat eaters. *Eoraptor* may have eaten meat but also ate plants. Fossils of herbivorous (plant-eating) dinosaurs from the same period have been found on the island of Madagascar.

Eoraptor.

EARTH DURING THE TRIASSIC

The early Triassic saw the continued existence of Pangea and a slow recovery from massive extinctions in the period before the Triassic. The world rapidly became populated by large numbers of individuals of relatively few species, so that there was little biological diversity. With Pangea straddling the Equator, much of the continent was hot and dry. Areas farther from the Equator probably had fairly harsh seasons, with hot summers and fairly cold winters, along with large seasonal differences in rainfall. In the late Triassic, Pangea began to break apart.

Herrerasaurus.

OTHER ANIMALS OF THE TRIASSIC

Therapsids (mammal-like reptiles) dominated animal life in the south, while primitive reptiles known as archosaurs were predominant in the north. The sea harbored an abundance of fish as well as newly evolved aquatic reptiles such as ichthyosaurs. The small shrewlike animals that were the first mammals also appeared late in the period. They are thought to have descended from the therapsids.

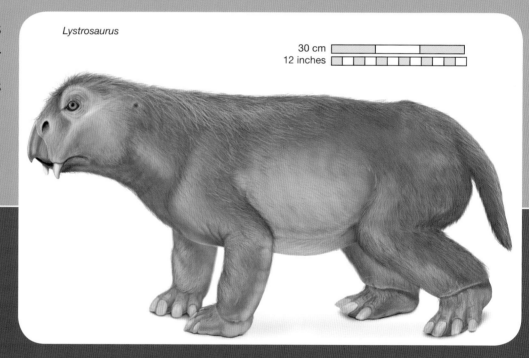

Lystrosaurus

30 cm
12 inches

Therapsids such as *Lystrosaurus* were mammal-like reptiles that thrived early in the Triassic Period.

END-TRIASSIC EXTINCTION

Scientists think that the mass extinction that occurred at the end of the Triassic Period (about 200 million years ago) may have been caused by rapid climate change or by an asteroid striking the Earth. This mass extinction event caused about 20 percent of marine families and some 76 percent of all extant species (those species living at that time) to die out—possibly within a span of about 10,000 years. This vast loss of species opened up many ecological niches, paving the way for the evolution of the dinosaurs.

THE
JURASSIC PERIOD

The Jurassic saw a continuation of the breakup of Pangea. The rifts between the splitting continents became shallow seas, and rising sea levels flooded parts of the continents. Reefs grew in the seas. The climate was generally warmer than today. Forests grew where Australia and Antarctica began to separate, eventually becoming coal deposits.

DINOSAURS OF THE JURASSIC

The dinosaurs greatly diversified in the Jurassic period. Some species reached enormous sizes, with plant-eating sauropods such as *Brachiosaurus* growing up to 40 feet (12 meters) tall and weighing up to 80 tons. The herbivores were preyed upon by carnivorous theropods such as *Allosaurus*. Some herbivores, such as *Stegosaurus*, developed self-defense features such as armored plates and bony spikes.

Allosaurus.

Conifers and ginkgos were common plants, and cycads were very abundant.

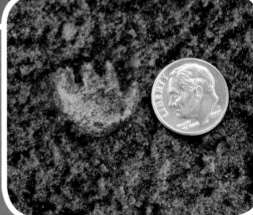

Scientists believe a small mammal left this track 190 million years ago in the area that is now Dinosaur National Monument.

Brachiosaurus.

BRACHIOSAURUS: **FIVE FAST FACTS**

1 *Brachiosaurus* ranks among the largest sauropods—and all land animals—that ever lived. It grew to approximately 75 feet (23 meters) in length and probably weighed between 55 and 66 tons.

2 It stood approximately 20 feet (6 meters) tall at the shoulders and its neck measured roughly 28 feet (8.5 meters) long, resulting in a total height of about 40 feet (12 meters).

3 The first fossil evidence of *Brachiosaurus* was collected in 1900 in the United States.

4 Bones from a pelvis, vertebral column, shoulder, ribs, and legs were taken from the Morrison rock formation in western Colorado.

5 Despite its size, scientists have speculated that it was capable of moving at speeds of about 12 to 19 miles per hour (19 to 31 kilometers per hour).

OTHER ANIMALS

The featherless flying and gliding reptiles called pterosaurs were common. *Archaeopteryx lithographica,* the oldest known animal that is generally accepted as a bird, first appeared in the late Jurassic. Mammals existed during this period as well but remained small.

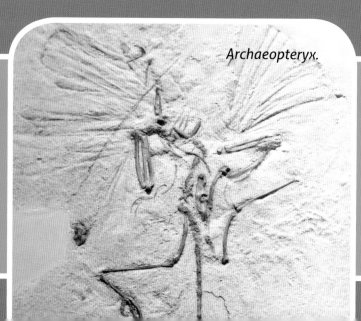

Archaeopteryx.

THE CRETACEOUS PERIOD

During the Cretaceous period, the Atlantic Ocean widened. The southern continent of Gondwana broke apart completely, and the equatorial Tethys Sea began to narrow as Africa drifted north toward Europe. India moved north toward Asia. The climate was warm, perhaps in part because of the way the continents were distributed but also likely from high levels of carbon dioxide released in the air from frequent volcanic activity. Forests, rather than ice, were to be found in the Arctic and Antarctic regions. The Cretaceous also saw a major change in plant evolution with the first appearance of the angiosperms, or flowering plants.

OCEANS

Thick deposits of chalk—the bodies of countless shell-producing marine organisms—were laid down in the shallow seas. Much of the deep ocean was largely devoid of life, though, as poor ocean circulation deprived the depths of oxygen. Large reptiles, such as plesiosaurs, swam in the sea.

The name Cretaceous is derived from the Latin word *creta*, meaning "chalk." This refers to a soft fine-grained limestone that was deposited in vast quantities during the late Cretaceous.

An artist's rendering of *Tyrannosaurs rex* and *Quetzalcoatlus.*

DINOSAURS

Dinosaurs in general became even more diversified in the Cretaceous period. Important theropods of this period included the fearsome *Tyrannosaurus rex, Velociraptor,* and *Oviraptor.* Two of the best studied herbivorous dinosaurs of the Cretaceous were the armored *Ankylosaurus* and the great horned *Triceratops.*

OTHER ANIMALS

Flying reptiles such as the pterodactyls were common but declining in number, with the huge *Pteranodon* and *Quetzalcoatlus* remaining until the end of the period. Primitive birds continued to evolve from the theropod dinosaurs.

Fairly modern reptiles, such as crocodiles and turtles, are seen in Cretaceous strata. Mammals developed into all three of their current groups: placentals, marsupials, and monotremes. The dinosaurs still dominated, though, and mammals remained quite small; many mammals of this period were burrowers that spent much of their time underground.

Members of the magnolia, laurel, sycamore, and rose families began to evolve during the Cretaceous period.

THE END OF AN ERA

The Cretaceous ended rather suddenly about 66 million years ago with a major extinction event that caused the end of the dinosaurs. While not quite as severe as the extinction event that preceded the Triassic, this extinction is one of the worst known, with nearly 80 percent of all species destroyed.

SAUROPODOMORPHA

Sauropodomorpha consists of two groups of plant-eating dinosaurs—Prosauropoda and Sauropoda. The dinosaurs of Prosauropoda may have been the ancestors of those of Sauropoda. The dinosaurs of both these groups had a small head and a long and well-muscled neck. Most of them walked on four legs. The largest dinosaurs and the largest land animals ever to live were sauropods; some grew to more than 100 feet (30 meters) in length. The sauropods had long necks and tails and elephant-like bodies and legs.

PROSAUROPODS: FIVE FAST FACTS

1. The prosauropods were perhaps the most widespread of all the Triassic dinosaurs—prosauropod fossils have been uncovered on every continent except Australia.

2. All prosauropods were herbivores, and most were quadrupeds, though some could move on their hind legs.

3. The most primitive of the herbivorous saurischians, the prosauropods ranged in length from 5 to 30 feet (1.5 to 9 meters). Prosauropods lived during the period from the late Triassic into the early Jurassic.

4. With their long necks and small heads, prosauropods foreshadowed the great sauropods that were soon to evolve.

5. The best studied prosauropod is *Plateosaurus*, a European herbivore that was 27 feet (8 meters) long and could walk on either two or four legs.

Plateosaurus.

SAUROPODS: FIVE FAST FACTS

1 As a group, the sauropods were remarkably long-lived. Their remains have been found in fossil beds dating from the late Triassic through the early Cretaceous periods—a time span of more than 100 million years.

2 Their true heyday, however, was the mid-Jurassic period, roughly 180 million years ago, when they diversified as a group and became widely distributed across the globe. Remains of these animals have been found on every continent.

3 Their spine was hollowed out at the sides, providing structural strength while remaining relatively lightweight.

4 Because of their size, most sauropods most likely had a distinct feeding advantage over other land-dwelling dinosaurs—their extremely long necks enabled them to browse among the tops of the tallest trees.

5 Unlike most herbivores, which generally have extremely strong teeth that help to grind the tough cellulose and lignin in plants, the teeth of most sauropods were relatively weak. Fossil evidence has revealed, however, that the sauropods had a strategy that enabled them to overcome this deficiency—they swallowed small stones, which helped them grind up the plant matter in their stomachs.

The family Camarasauridae contains smaller sauropods with shorter necks and tails than most other species. The most familiar member is *Camarasaurus*.

Gastroliths were stones that settled in the stomach and helped sauropods to grind up the tough plant material they consumed.

SAUROPODS IN THE SPOTLIGHT

APATOSAURUS

Apatosaurus grew to about 70 feet (21 meters) in length, measured roughly 15 feet (4.6 meters) tall at the hips, and weighed an estimated 30 to 36 tons. Its relatively thick neck was about 20 feet (about 6.1 meters) long, but its head was small in relation to its body, measuring only 2 feet (61 centimeters) in length. Its heavy, powerful tail was even longer than its neck.

Apatosaurus.

FAST FACTS

1. Trackways of sauropod dinosaurs at fossil sites suggest that *Apatosaurus* may have traveled in herds.

2. Its diet is thought to have included the twigs and needles of sequoia, fir, and pine trees.

3. The first fossil evidence of *Apatosaurus*, a hipbone, was collected in 1877 in the United States near Morrison, Colo. The genus was first described and named in 1887.

Jobaria.

JOBARIA

A huge herbivorous dinosaur, *Jobaria* inhabited parts of Saharan Africa approximately 135 million years ago during the Cretaceous period (144–65 million years ago). Although *Jobaria* closely resembles members of the Sauropoda, it is classified in a distinct lineage of sauropod ancestors that thrived and endured exclusively in northern Africa during the Cretaceous period.

A nearly complete (95 percent) skeleton was the first fossil evidence of *Jobaria*. It was discovered by paleontologist Paul Sereno and his team during a 1997 fossil-hunting expedition. Along with this nearly complete skeleton, Sereno and his team uncovered a mass burial site containing several adult and juvenile *Jobaria* specimens. What caused the group's apparently sudden demise is a mystery. One theory holds that an ancient flash flood may have rapidly engulfed the dinosaurs, though it is possible that some individuals were killed by the predatory *Afrovenator*.

SEISMOSAURUS

Seismosaurus inhabited western North America during the late Jurassic period, approximately 159 to 144 million years ago. *Seismosaurus* may have been the longest species of dinosaur to ever exist. Fossil evidence shows that some individuals measured more than 150 feet (46 meters) long—equal to half the length of a U.S. football playing field. The tremendous size of its hips and sacrum, which supported its massive body as it walked, indicates that the dinosaur would have weighed approximately 100 tons or more, rivaling in size the largest living animal on Earth—the blue whale.

Seismosaurus.

THEROPODA

A subcategory of the lizard-hipped dinosaur order Saurischia, the Theropoda includes all carnivorous, or meat-eating, dinosaurs. The theropods were a highly diverse group that ranged in size from the relatively small 100-pound (45-kilogram) *Velociraptor*, to the massive 6-ton *Tyrannosaurus rex*. Fossil evidence indicates that modern birds share a common ancestor with a branch of the theropods.

Afrovenator, a fearsome predator that inhabited the continent of Africa approximately 130 million years ago during the Cretaceous period (144–65 million years ago).

FIVE FAST FACTS

1 All theropods were bipedal, meaning that they stood upright and ran or walked on their two hind limbs.

2 Their legs were long and muscular; in many species, the tibia, or shin bone, was longer than the femur, or thigh bone.

3 Theropods had fairly short arms that ended in grasping hands armed with two or three clawed fingers, depending upon the species.

4 Like modern birds, most species of theropods had hollow bones.

5 Theropods are most noted for the rows of razor-sharp teeth that lined their powerful jaws, enabling them to tear the flesh of their prey easily.

From the size of its massive skull, which measured approximately 5.4 feet (1.6 meters) long, paleontologists estimate that *Carcharodontosaurus* probably reached a length of more than 45 feet (13.7 meters).

CARNOSAURS AND TYRANNOSAURS

The most ferocious predators during the Jurassic period (approximately 201–145 million years ago) were the Carnosauria. This group of dinosaurs was a sub-category of the Theropoda. The most notable carnosaur was *Allosaurus*, which appeared during the late Jurassic period, about 145 to 163 million years ago. It could reach a length of up to 39 feet (12 meters) and weighed approximately 1.5 tons. Other species of carnosaurs included the megalosaurs, some of which could reach a length of up to 30 feet (9 meters). By the late Cretaceous period, about 65 to 80 million years ago, carnosaurs were replaced by the tyrannosaurs. This group included the *Tyrannosaurus rex* ("tyrant lizard king"). This formidable beast reached a length of 42 feet (12.8 meters) and weighed up to 8 tons.

Allosaurus.

THEROPODA:
SMALL BUT DANGEROUS

ORNITHOMIMUS

Ornithomimus was a small, birdlike dinosaur that inhabited North America and Asia about 65 to 98 million years ago during the late Cretaceous period. *Ornithomimus* is classified as a member of the family Ornithomimidae, which contains ostrichlike dinosaurs with exceptionally large eyes and brains.

FAST FACTS

1. *Ornithomimus* grew to about 12 feet (3.7 meters) in length and stood roughly 8 feet (2.4 meters) tall.

2. Although the head was light and small, the brain was large, earning *Ornithomimus* a reputation as one of the most intelligent of the dinosaurs.

3. *Ornithomimus* presumably was a swift runner, perhaps reaching speeds up to 30 miles per hour (48 kilometers per hour) while pursuing prey or escaping enemies.

4. Although classified among the carnivorous theropods, *Ornithomimus* was probably omnivorous, consuming plants and fruit in addition to insects and small animals such as lizards. It also may have raided nests and eaten dinosaur eggs, using its beak to break the shells.

Ornithomimus.

COMPSOGNATHUS

Compsognathus was a small, carnivorous dinosaur that inhabited Europe during the late Jurassic period, about 144 to 163 million years ago. It is the sole member of the family Compsognathidae, which belongs to the lizard-hipped dinosaur order, Saurischia.

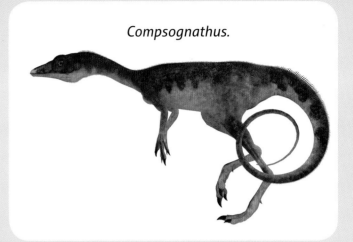
Compsognathus.

FAST FACTS

1. *Compsognathus* was one of the smallest of all dinosaurs, standing no higher than a chicken, and was similar in structure to *Archaeopteryx*, the first known bird.

2. The jaw contained many small, sharp teeth, which gave this dinosaur its name: *Compsognathus* means "pretty jaw."

3. The first fossil evidence of *Compsognathus* was an essentially complete skeleton discovered in Bavaria in southern Germany in the late 1850s. The remains of a young *Bavarisaurus*—a small, fleet lizard—were found in its stomach cavity, attesting to the speed and agility of *Compsognathus*.

OVIRAPTOR

Oviraptor was a small, carnivorous dinosaur that inhabited Asia during the late Cretaceous period, about 65 to 98 million years ago. *Oviraptor* is classified as a member of the family Oviraptoridae, a small family of toothless dinosaurs.

Oviraptor.

FAST FACTS

1. *Oviraptor* had a distinctive, lightweight skull unique among the dinosaurs. Its head resembled that of a parrot—deep and short with a toothless, stumpy beak.

2. The curved jaws were heavily muscled, providing the beak with the power to crush hard objects such as bones. Scientists believe that *Oviraptor* may have fed mainly on mollusks, using its beak to crush the shells.

THEROPODA:
BRAINS AND CLAWS

VELOCIRAPTOR

Velociraptor was an agile carnivorous dinosaur that inhabited Asia during the late Cretaceous period, approximately 65 to 99 million years ago. *Velociraptor* is classified as a member of the family Dromaeosauridae, which includes dinosaurs with an especially large and deadly sickle-shaped claw.

FAST FACTS

1. *Velociraptor* was a small dinosaur, averaging only about 6 feet (2 meters) in length and weighing approximately 100 pounds (45 kilograms).

2. The quickness, agility, and lightweight body of *Velociraptor* made it one of the top predators of its time. A fairly intelligent dinosaur, its large brain enabled it to make complex maneuvers when chasing prey.

3. *Velociraptor* preyed mainly upon herbivores that were smaller than itself. It also hunted in packs in order to bring down larger dinosaurs. *Velociraptor* was primarily an ambush predator and leapt out upon its prey in a surprise attack from behind the cover of vegetation.

Velociraptor.

DEINONYCHUS

Deinonychus was a carnivorous dinosaur that inhabited North America during the early Cretaceous period, approximately 98 to 144 million years ago. *Deinonychus* is classified in the family Dromaeosauridae.

Deinonychus.

FAST FACTS

① As a predator, *Deinonychus* was built for the chase and the kill. Its body was strong and light; the average individual probably measured 10 feet (3 meters) in length and 6 feet (1.8 meters) in height and weighed only 150 pounds (68 kilograms).

② On each foot, the second of four toes had a long claw shaped like a sickle, which was presumably used to slash through the flesh of prey. The claw measured up to 5 inches (13 centimeters). This attribute inspired the name *Deinonychus*, which means "terrible claw."

TROODON

A small carnivorous dinosaur, *Troodon* inhabited North America during the late Cretaceous period, approximately 99 to 65 million years ago. *Troodon* is classified as a member of the family Troodontidae.

FAST FACTS

① Paleontologists consider *Troodon* to be among the most intelligent of dinosaurs.

② The most distinguishing feature of *Troodon* was its very large, partly forward-facing eyes. This unique adaptation may have enabled the animal to have binocular vision, or overlapping fields of vision, similar to that of modern humans.

③ Because *Troodon*'s large eyes would have provided it with excellent vision in low-light situations, paleontologists conclude that this dinosaur hunted primarily at night while lurking in the dark forests.

THEROPODA:
LARGE PREDATORS

MEGALOSAURUS

Megalosaurus was a large, carnivorous dinosaur that inhabited Britain about 161 to 176 million years ago, during the Jurassic period. *Megalosaurus* is classified as a member of the family Megalosauridae. *Megalosaurus* was one of the first dinosaurs to be discovered and the first to be described and named. The first fossil evidence of *Megalosaurus*—some vertebrae and parts of a jaw, shoulder, hip, and leg—was discovered in the early 1800s. When it was first described in 1824, it was given the name *Megalosaurus*, meaning "great lizard." *Megalosaurus* reached a length of about 30 feet (9 meters), a height of 10 feet (3 meters), and an estimated weight of one ton.

Megalosaurus.

ALLOSAURUS

A large carnivorous dinosaur, *Allosaurus* was a fierce predator that inhabited North America and probably Africa, Australia, and Asia during the late Jurassic period, approximately 144 to 159 million years ago. *Allosaurus* is classified as a member of the family Allosauridae. *Allosaurus* grew up to 39 feet (12 meters) in length, weighed approximately 1.5 tons, and stood about 15 feet (4.5 meters) tall. Its head was massive, measuring 3 feet (91 centimeters) in length, but fairly light in weight because of several large open spaces within the skull bones. Despite its size, paleontologists believe that *Allosaurus* was a speedy, agile predator capable of hunting down enormous herbivorous dinosaurs.

SEE *ALLOSAURUS* IN THE VR APP!

CERATOSAURUS

Ceratosaurus was a large carnivorous dinosaur that inhabited North America about 144 to 163 million years ago during the late Jurassic period. *Ceratosaurus* is classified as a member of the family Ceratosauridae. *Ceratosaurus* lived at the same time as its relative, *Allosaurus*. *Ceratosaurus* was close in size to *Allosaurus*, with some *Ceratosaurus* specimens reaching up to 30 feet (9 meters) in length and 6.5 feet (2 meters) in height. The most unusual feature of *Ceratosaurus* was a row of bony plates just below the skin along the top of the neck, body, and tail. The purpose of the plates is unclear, but some scientists speculate that they might have functioned as a courtship or dominance display.

Ceratosaurus.

THEROPODA:
THE TITAN OF TERROR

The *Tyrannosaurus rex* was a large, carnivorous dinosaur that inhabited North America approximately 65 to 98 million years ago during the late Cretaceous period. The most widely recognized of all the dinosaurs, *T. rex* has inspired much speculation about how it lived, as well as what and how it ate. Although once thought to belong to the ferocious Carnosauria ("flesh-eating lizards"), the *T. rex* is now classified as a gigantic member of the Coelurosauria ("hollow-tailed lizards").

A *T. rex* skull.

A *T. rex* tooth.

JUST THE STATS

The largest specimen ever found has a body length of 40 feet (12 meters) from head to tail and may have weighed more than four tons. The elongated head was massive, measuring roughly 5 feet (1.5 meters) in length. The jaws were powerfully muscled, and the huge mouth contained two rows of serrated, pointed teeth, many measuring about 6 inches (15 centimeters) long, though some may have reached as much as 12 inches (30 centimeters) in length.

HUNTER OR SCAVENGER?

A good deal of scientific debate has focused on *T. rex*'s methods of obtaining prey. One school of thought is that it was a scavenger, an animal that searches for and consumes prey that is already dead. The evidence offered in support of this hypothesis includes the small size of the animal's eyes (suggesting poor vision), the enormous size and bulk (which may have prevented it from obtaining the high speeds necessary for chasing down a variety of prey), and the large olfactory bulbs in its skull. This latter feature indicates that the part of *T. rex*'s brain used for olfaction, or smell, was enlarged, indicating that this trait was selected for because it was adaptive. Organisms that possess traits that are adaptive tend to thrive at the expense of other, less well-adapted individuals. From an evolutionary perspective, an enhanced sense of smell is advantageous to a scavenger. Modern scavengers, such as vultures, have enlarged olfactory lobes.

A second group of researchers believe that *T. rex* was a true predator, capable of chasing down and killing its prey. This group cites the example of modern predators such as lions and hyenas, which scavenge carcasses when faced with no other choice but appear to prefer tracking down and consuming fresh meat.

Was *T. rex* a hunter or a scavenger? These illustrations depict very different possibilities.

CERAPODA: ORNITHOPODA

Scientists divide the Ornithischia into two suborders: the Thyreophora and the Cerapoda. The Cerapoda consists of three groups: Ornithopoda, Ceratopsia, and Pachycephalosauria.

The Ornithopoda includes the small heterodontosaurs and hypsilophodontids, the much larger iguanodonts, and the large duck-billed hadrosaurs. The ornithopods were an exceptionally successful group from an evolutionary perspective, surviving the entire Jurassic and Cretaceous periods—a span of almost 150 million years.

IGUANODON

A large, herbivorous dinosaur that inhabited North America, Europe, Africa, and Asia during the early Cretaceous period, about 98 to 144 million years ago. *Iguanodon* is classified as a member of the family Iguanodontidae, which contains bulky, fairly slow-moving dinosaurs.

Iguanodon grew to about 30 feet (9 meters) in length, stood over 15 feet (4.6 meters) tall, and probably weighed about 5 tons. Its skeletal structure and other evidence indicate that it probably spent most of its time grazing on all four limbs but was capable of rearing up on its hind legs to browse in trees. Its head ended in a broad, toothless beak that it may have used to clip plant material, which was then pushed back for grinding by the blunt teeth in its powerful jaws. *Iguanodon*'s teeth resembled those of the modern iguana and inspired its name, which means "iguana tooth."

Iguanodon was the second dinosaur to be discovered, nearly 20 years before Richard Owen coined the name "dinosaur." Gideon Mantell, a British physician and avid geologist, found the first fossil evidence of *Iguanodon* in southern England in the early 1820s.

LESOTHOSAURUS

Lesothosaurus was a small, herbivorous dinosaur that inhabited Africa during the early Jurassic period, about 176 to 201 million years ago. A member of the family Fabrosauridae, which contains small, lizardlike dinosaurs, *Lesothosaurus* is the earliest known member of the order Ornithischia (the bird-hipped dinosaurs).

Lesothosaurus was a small dinosaur, measuring just over 3 feet (0.9 meter) in length. The skull was small and flat-faced, resembling that of an iguana. The pointed teeth, which were shaped like small arrowheads, had grooved edges. The jaws were well adapted for dealing with tough vegetation.

CERAPODA:
ORNITHOPODA

Hypsilophodon.

HYPSILOPHODON

A small, herbivorous dinosaur that inhabited Europe and North America during the early Cretaceous period, about 98 to 144 million years ago, *Hypsilophodon* is classified as a member of the family Hypsilophodontidae. These were among the most successful of the dinosaurs, flourishing for roughly 100 million years from the late Jurassic through the early Cretaceous periods. *Hypsilophodon* grew to approximately 5 feet (1.5 meters) in length, stood about 3 feet (0.9 meter) tall, and weighed about 140 pounds (64 kilograms).

Fossil evidence suggests that the hypsilophodonts were social animals that lived in herds. Their lightweight bodies and long legs suggest that they were able to sprint from predators, earning them a reputation as the "gazelles" of the dinosaurs.

ORODROMEUS

Orodromeus was a small, herbivorous dinosaur that inhabited North America during the late Cretaceous period, about 65 to 98 million years ago. *Orodromeus* is classified as a member of the family Hypsilophodontidae.

The first fossil evidence of *Orodromeus* was discovered in the 1980s while a crew of paleontologists was examining nests of hadrosaur dinosaurs in Montana. At nearby sites that were later dubbed Egg Mountain and Egg Island, they discovered a large number of eggs of a new ornithopod dinosaur among the hadrosaur remains. The new dinosaur was named *Orodromeus*, which means "mountain runner," because of both the location of the find and the animal's presumed swiftness, based on its long hind limbs and slender build. The eggs and nests were remarkably well preserved; one complete nest contained 19 eggs laid in a precise spiral.

Orodromeus.

HETERODONTOSAURUS

Heterodontosaurus was a small, herbivorous dinosaur that inhabited areas of South Africa during the Jurassic Period, about 200 million years ago. *Heterodontosaurus* was a small dinosaur, measuring about 3 feet (1 meter) in length and weighing up to 5.5 pounds (2.5 kilograms).

The distinguishing feature of *Heterodontosaurus* was its teeth, of which it had three different types. The first type of teeth were small and sharp and were located in the front of its top jaw. Its bottom jaw formed a horny beak in the front. The second type of teeth were long canine tusks that grew out of the top and bottom jaws. The third type of teeth were square-shaped cheek teeth in the back, similar to molars in modern mammals. With these different teeth, *Heterodontosaurus* could tear, bite, and grind its food. This dinosaur also had large cheek pouches.

Heterodontosaurus.

CERAPODA:
THE HADROSAURS

The Hadrosauridae are often called the duck-billed dinosaurs because the skulls of some species were broad and flat in front like a duck's bill. The hadrosaurs had rows of very tough teeth, as many as 500 to 2,000 teeth in the skull, depending on the species. The hadrosaurs can be divided into two groups—those with skull crests and those without. Both groups lived during the mid- to late Cretaceous.

A hadrosaur footprint in Colorado.

SHANTUNGOSAURUS

Shantungosaurus from China was the largest of the noncrested hadrosaurs. It was 49 feet (15 meters) long from its bill to the tip of its tail. Hadrosaur fossils have been found in rocks that were laid down in moist, swampy places, suggesting that this group may have spent some time browsing for water plants in swamps as do modern moose.

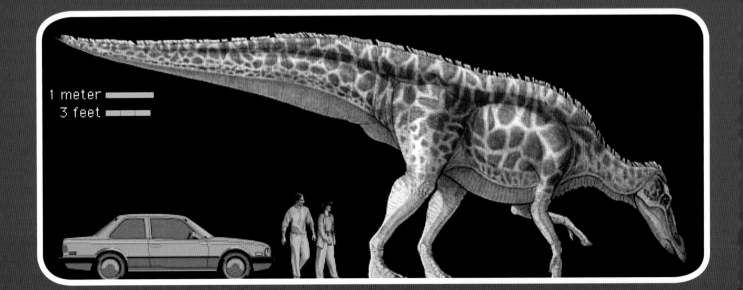

1 meter
3 feet

MAIASAURA

Studies of one of the best-known noncrested hadrosaurs, *Maiasaura*, have produced key insights about parental care among dinosaurs. An adult female *Maiasaura* averaged 30 feet (9 meters) in length—too large to brood eggs by sitting on them. Some scientists have proposed that adults spread vegetation over the nested eggs. As the plant matter rotted, fermentation produced heat, thus incubating the eggs in a manner similar to that used by modern crocodiles.

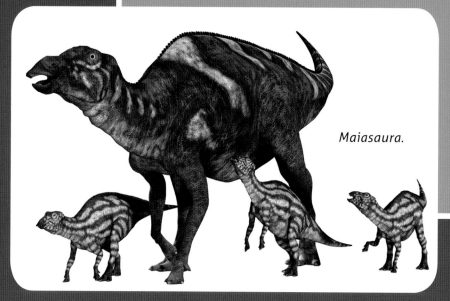

Maiasaura.

THE CRESTED HADROSAURS

The crested duck-billed dinosaurs were an unusual group of animals mainly from North America. They sported a variety of crests on the tops of their heads, through which the nasal passages passed. These crests ranged from the rounded crest of *Corythosaurus*, to the hatchet-shaped crest of a *Lambeosaurus* species, to the long, curved crest of *Parasaurolophus*. The crests may have functioned to amplify territorial or courtship calls. It is clear, from their unusual skeletons and fossil evidence of parental care, that these dinosaurs were highly evolved, complex animals.

Lambeosaurus.

Parasaurolophus.

The name *Corythosaurus* means "helmet lizard."

CERAPODA: CERATOPSIA AND PACHYCEPHALOSAURIA

Ceratopsia and Pachycephalosauria are sometimes grouped together as the Marginocephalia because they share several features.

PACHYCEPHALOSAURIA

The pachycephalosaurs are commonly called the bone-headed, or dome-headed, dinosaurs. Their name derives from their unusually thick skulls, which formed a rounded dome on their foreheads. Paleontologists once proposed that these domes enabled the animals to use their heads as battering rams in contests with one another, much in the way that modern bighorn sheep do. However, later studies revealed that the domes were inadequate for this task and were better adapted for butting rivals and adversaries in the flank. Most pachycephalosaurs were bipedal, and some were quite large. The largest was *Pachycephalosaurus*, which had a wall of bone over the top of its brain case that was 10 inches (25 centimeters) thick.

Pachycephalosaurus inhabited North America during the late Cretaceous period, about 65 to 98 million years ago.

Pachycephalosaurus.

Psittacosaurus.

CERATOPSIA

The Ceratopsia are called the horned dinosaurs, though some of the earliest ceratopsids lacked horns. Ceratopsids lived during the Cretaceous period. All were herbivorous, and the fossil evidence suggests that most species lived in herds.

The hornless ceratopsids make up the family Protoceratopsidae, which includes the human-sized bipedal *Psittacosaurus* from Mongolia, named for its unusual parrot-shaped head. Although they lacked horns, both *Leptoceratops* from western North America and *Protoceratops* from Asia had neck frills, though that of Leptoceratops was fairly small. The latter, which could walk on two legs or four, was about 8 feet (2.4 meters) long. The quadrupedal *Protoceratops* was roughly the same size; fossil specimens suggest that adults were roughly 6 to 8 feet (1.8 to 2.4 meters) in length.

Scientists have long speculated about the function of the ceratopsids' horns and neck frills. It is thought that though both features may have played a role in defense, they also served other functions. Like modern horned mammals such as sheep and buffalo, the ceratopsids probably used their horns mainly in fights and displays with each other, as in contests for dominance or mates. Studies of the neck frills suggest that these functioned largely in regulating body temperature, in much the same way as did the bony plates of stegosaurids.

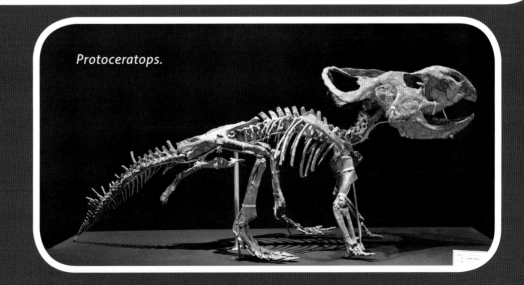

Protoceratops.

CERATOPSIDS
IN THE SPOTLIGHT

TRICERATOPS

The most famous ceratopsid was *Triceratops*. These dinosaurs were up to 30 feet (9 meters) long, weighed up to 6 tons, and had the largest heads of any land animals ever. *Triceratops* had a monstrous beak, dozens of teeth for grinding plants, three long sharp horns, and a thick shield of bone over the neck. This dinosaur was built like a rhinoceros, but unlike those mostly solitary animals, *Triceratops* and its relatives probably lived in groups. North America was the home of most of these animals, and during the Cretaceous period they may have roamed like migrating herds of modern bison.

FIVE FAST FACTS

① The name *Triceratops*, which means "three-horned face," was inspired by the animal's most striking feature. Projecting from its massive skull—which measured more than 6 feet (2 meters) in length—were three sharp horns.

② The two upper horns, one projecting above each eye, reached a length of more than 3 feet (1 meter). The third horn projected from the animal's snout.

③ Fossil evidence strongly suggests these horns were used in harmless contests of strength—many of the neck frills found display scars where they had been scored by the horns of other *Triceratops*.

④ The dinosaurs seem to have locked horns and pushed against one another's head frills, in much the same way that modern deer compete for mates by clashing antlers.

⑤ *Triceratops* browsed among the flowering plants, low-hanging coniferous tree branches, and shrubs that were present during the late Cretaceous period.

Centrosaurus was a large, herbivorous dinosaur that inhabited North America during the late Cretaceous period, approximately 65 to 98 million years ago.

Centrosaurus bone beds uncovered in the Red Deer River valley in the Canadian province of Alberta support the idea that this dinosaur may have grazed and traveled in herds.

THYREOPHORA

The dinosaurs of the subgroup Thyreophora were either plated or armored. Plated dinosaurs such as *Stegosaurus* had a double row of upright triangular bony plates running down the back. *Ankylosaurus* and other armored dinosaurs had flattened armor all over the top and sides of their bodies. Their armor did not form a shell like a turtle's, but it was probably just as effective.

ANKYLOSAURUS

Ankylosaurus was a large armored dinosaur that inhabited North America approximately 70 million to 66 million years ago during the Late Cretaceous Period. It grew to a length of about 33 feet (10 meters) and weighed approximately four tons. *Ankylosaurus* was a quadruped, meaning that it walked on four legs, which on this dinosaur were short but thick and strong. Its head, which measured about 2.5 feet (76 centimeters) long, was broader than it was long. The head, body, and tail were covered with bony plates set in leathery skin. Two sets of large spikes projected from the head, and rows of short spikes ran along the sides and tail. The tail, which was as long as the body, ended in a heavy "club" of bone, which it probably swung as a defense against predators.

Ankylosaurus.

SCELIDOSAURUS

An armored herbivorous dinosaur, *Scelidosaurus* inhabited parts of Europe during the early Jurassic period, approximately 206–180 million years ago. It is a member of the family Scelidosauridae.

Scelidosaurus' physical characteristics have led some paleontologists to argue that it was a primitive stegosaur, and thus an early ancestor of the plated dinosaur *Stegosaurus*. Others suggest that it was more closely related to the ankylosaurs such as *Ankylosaurus*. Most experts agree, however, that *Scelidosaurus* was among the common ancestors of both groups.

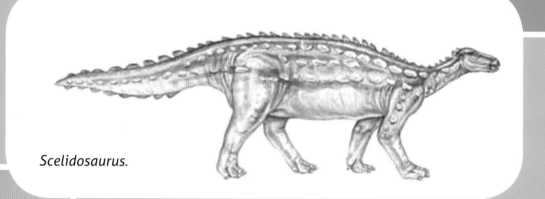

Scelidosaurus.

EUOPLOCEPHALUS

Euoplocephalus was a large herbivorous dinosaur that inhabited North America during the Late Cretaceous Period, approximately 100 million to 66 million years ago. *Euoplocephalus* is classified in the infraorder Ankylosauria, which contains heavily armored dinosaurs distinguished by well-developed head armor and clublike tails. *Euoplocephalus* was a powerfully built tanklike creature that grew to about 20 feet (6 meters) in length and probably weighed more than two tons.

Euoplocephalus.

STEGOSAURUS IN THE SPOTLIGHT

In the Jurassic period, the main group of armored dinosaurs was the Stegosauria. Stegosaurid fossils have been found on every continent except Antarctica, Australia, and South America. The most familiar of the stegosaurids is *Stegosaurus*.

WHAT WAS IT LIKE?

Stegosaurus normally reached an average length of 21 feet (6.5 meters), but some individuals grew to 30 feet (9 meters). *Stegosaurus* weighed approximately 2 tons and stood about 12 feet (3.7 meters) tall at the hips. *Stegosaurus* had a horn-covered beak instead of front teeth, and its cheek teeth had ridged surfaces made for grinding plant material. The tail of *Stegosaurus* was armed with two pairs of spikes that measured up to 3 feet (1 meter) in length. This dinosaur carried its tail high above the ground.

NOT THAT SMART

The skull and brain of *Stegosaurus* were especially small for such a large animal. Its narrow head measured only 16 inches (40 centimeters) long. There once was a mistaken belief that this dinosaur had two brains because the sacrum region of the spinal cord was actually larger than its brain cavity. Recent theories suggest, however, that the sacrum region may have been used to store glycogen, which contains carbohydrates, as it does in several modern animals.

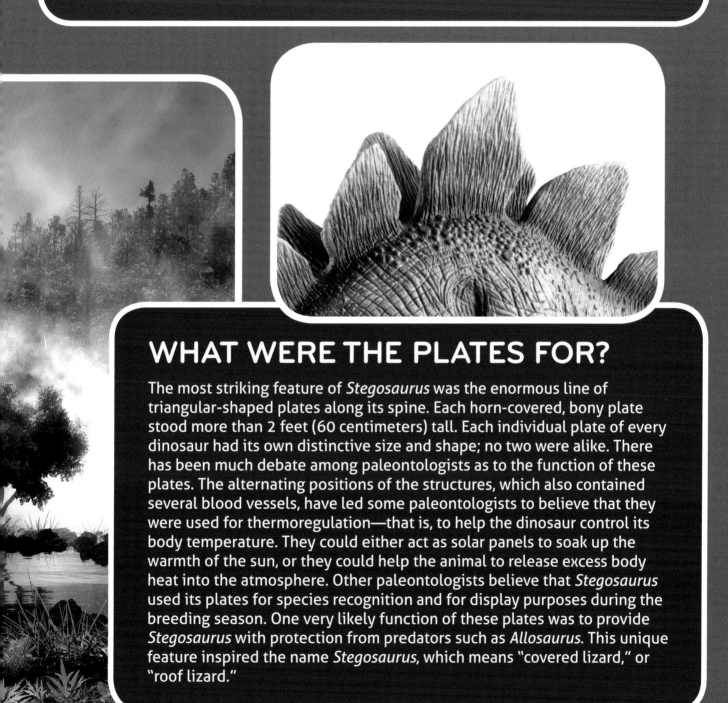

WHAT WERE THE PLATES FOR?

The most striking feature of *Stegosaurus* was the enormous line of triangular-shaped plates along its spine. Each horn-covered, bony plate stood more than 2 feet (60 centimeters) tall. Each individual plate of every dinosaur had its own distinctive size and shape; no two were alike. There has been much debate among paleontologists as to the function of these plates. The alternating positions of the structures, which also contained several blood vessels, have led some paleontologists to believe that they were used for thermoregulation—that is, to help the dinosaur control its body temperature. They could either act as solar panels to soak up the warmth of the sun, or they could help the animal to release excess body heat into the atmosphere. Other paleontologists believe that *Stegosaurus* used its plates for species recognition and for display purposes during the breeding season. One very likely function of these plates was to provide *Stegosaurus* with protection from predators such as *Allosaurus*. This unique feature inspired the name *Stegosaurus*, which means "covered lizard," or "roof lizard."

PREDATOR AND PREY

VELOCIRAPTOR VS. PROTOCERATOPS

Amazing fossil evidence of *Velociraptor* was discovered in Mongolia in 1971. This discovery confirmed paleontologists' theories about the method of attack used by *Velociraptor* and other dromaeosaurs. A complete skeleton of the predator was found locked in a battle to the death with the horned dinosaur *Protoceratops*. Both were apparently victims of a sudden sandstorm in the desert at the time of the attack. While grasping the head frill of *Protoceratops*, *Velociraptor* was in the process of slashing open the throat and underside of its victim with its sickle-claw. At the same time, *Protoceratops* had the right arm of *Velociraptor* locked securely in its beak-like jaws. This fossil discovery clearly ranks among the greatest and most dramatic finds in paleontology.

An artist's rendering of a confrontation between *Allosaurus* and *Apatosaurus*.

ALLOSAURUS VS. APATOSAURUS

Bones of the dinosaur *Apatosaurus* have been found with teeth marks from *Allosaurus*. Skeletal characteristics suggest that *Allosaurus* disabled its prey with its claws before using its teeth to carve out large portions.

An artist's rendering of *Stegosaurus* trying to fight off attackers.

STEGOSAURUS VS. THEROPOD

Stegosaurus may have used its spiked tail as a defensive weapon against predators. One powerful swing could have driven its deadly spikes deep into the flesh of any meat-eating theropod that chose to attack this otherwise peaceful plant eater.

COELOPHYSIS VS. COELOPHYSIS

Coelophysis was a small, carnivorous dinosaur that inhabited North America during the late Triassic period, about 208 to 230 million years ago. *Coelophysis* grew to a maximum length of approximately 10 feet (3 meters) and stood nearly 3 feet (0.9 meter) tall at its hips. Its weight and bone structure suggest that *Coelophysis* was swift and agile. Fossil evidence indicates that it lived and hunted in groups—perhaps families—in forests near streams and lakes. *Coelophysis* also may have scavenged from carcasses. Quarrying operations at Ghost Ranch in New Mexico in 1947 yielded the remains of several hundred individuals of varying sizes, suggesting that families may have lived together and then died together in some catastrophic event. The discovery of skeletal remains of juveniles inside the bodies of two adults led paleontologists to speculate that *Coelophysis* sometimes engaged in cannibalism.

Coelophysis.

DINOSAURS AND BIRDS

Many scientists believe that the closest dinosaur ancestors of birds belonged to a group of small carnivorous dinosaurs called coelurosaurs that evolved in the Jurassic period. Like modern birds, dinosaurs belonging to this group walked on their hind legs, and shared many other characteristics, such as long tails, three forward-pointing toes, and a similarly structured breastbone, or sternum.

DINOSAURS WITH FEATHERS

Several discoveries from the fossil-rich Liaoning Province in northeastern China provide strong support for a link between dinosaurs and birds. In the late 1990s a team of paleontologists discovered the fossil remains of three previously unknown dinosaurs that all had evidence of feathers. One nearly intact skeleton, later named *Sinosauropteryx*, also had a fertilized egg and the animal's fossilized oviduct—the first discovery of a fossilized internal organ from a dinosaur. The fossils' estimated age of 140 to 120 million years old places these dinosaurs in the late Jurassic or early Cretaceous periods.

In 2000, another expedition in Liaoning produced a small dinosaur that appeared even more closely related to birds. The crow-sized dinosaur, which scientists named *Microraptor zhaoianus*, lived in the late Jurassic or early Cretaceous periods.

Further excavations at the Liaoning site in 2002 produced specimens of another *Microraptor* species, which scientists named *M. gui*. Unlike previously discovered feathered dinosaurs, the *M. gui* specimens each had birdlike feathers on both hindlimbs and forelimbs. Experts propose that these four wings were well adapted for gliding, which some scientists hypothesize may have been an early step in the evolution of flight.

A report in 2014 revealed the first evidence of featherlike structures on a plant-eating dinosaur. The remains of *Kulindadromeus zabaikalicus*, a small dinosaur that lived in Siberia during the Jurassic period, showed the presence of filaments and featherlike structures on its limbs.

An artist's rendering of microraptors.

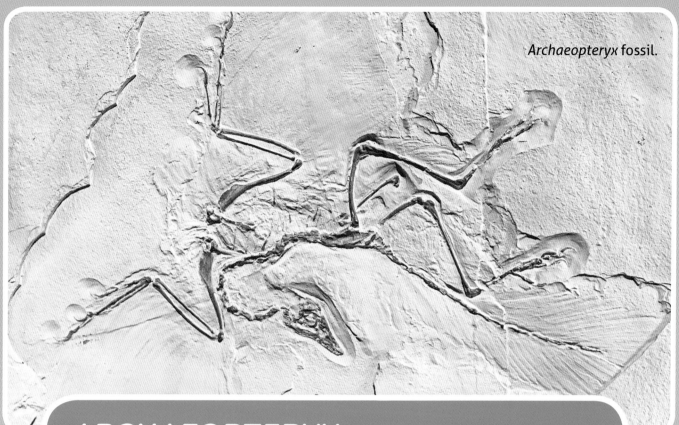

Archaeopteryx fossil.

ARCHAEOPTERYX

The famous Jurassic fossil of *Archaeopteryx* was once considered part dinosaur and part bird. Today scientists believe it was a true bird, perhaps one of the earliest known, and consider it a key link in the evolution between dinosaurs and birds. Recent discoveries in Liaoning have provided even closer links. Among these were the discovery in 1995 of a primitive bird known as *Confuciusornis*, which lived during the late Jurassic; and the 2002 discovery of another fossilized bird, which scientists named *Jeholornis*. The latter fossil is between 110 and 124 million years old, and had the strong beak and wings seen in modern birds. The fossil also had a stomach full of seeds, providing the first evidence of seed-eating among early birds.

Archaeopteryx.

SHARING THE WORLD OF DINOSAURS

Although dinosaurs were the most spectacular animals of their day, they were by no means alone on the Earth. Other reptiles walked the land, flew through the air, and swam in the water. There were birds, mammals, and some odd creatures that were halfway between the reptile and the mammal.

An artist's rendering of mosasaurs.

IN THE SEA

Mosasaurs, giant lizards that ranged from 16 to 33 feet (5 to 10 meters) in length, never left the sea. They had short paddles instead of legs and propelled themselves through the water by swinging their long tails from side to side.

An ichthyosaur.

Ichthyosaurs (meaning "fish-lizards"), smaller reptiles that lived entirely in the ocean, looked very much like sharks. Fossil evidence indicates that, like mammals, they gave birth to live young instead of laying eggs, as reptiles do.

Plesiosaurs were ocean-dwelling reptiles, most of which were about 15 feet (5 meters) long, though some later forms were as long as 43 feet (13 meters). Some species had very long necks and had flippers instead of legs.

An artist's rendering of a plesiosaur.

TURTLES

The earliest fossils recognized as turtles are about 200 million years old and date from the Triassic Period. Turtles have changed little in appearance since that time.

ON THE LAND

Theriodonts (meaning "mammal-toothed") were members of a reptile family that died out about 190 million years ago. They had skeletal features that suggest an evolutionary midpoint between the reptile and the mammal.

MORGANUCODON

Morganucodon is an extinct genus of tiny mammals that lived approximately 200 million years ago on the boundary between the Triassic and Jurassic geologic periods. *Morganucodon* was one of the earliest mammals.

Morganucodon weighed only about 1–3 ounces (27–89 grams) and probably ate insects and other small invertebrates. Like living mammals, *Morganucodon* had skin covered with hair. It also possessed a small gerbil-like or ratlike body and a long face similar to those of shrews or civets. In addition, the brain of *Morganucodon* was smaller than that of any living mammal. Its hearing, however, was sensitive to higher frequencies than that of contemporary birds and reptiles.

Morganucodon.

2 cm
1 inch

IN THE AIR

In the time of the dinosaurs, reptiles called pterosaurs sailed through the air. They glided from tree to tree and soared on air currents instead of actually flying, because they had no feathers. Their long wings were formed from membranes of skin, like those of modern bats. The wings were supported by the greatly lengthened fourth finger. The other fingers were hooked claws. Their legs were so weak that the animals probably could not perch or walk. Pterosaurs had long, slender beaks, and some had strong, sharply pointed teeth. One pterosaur was no larger than a sparrow.

The pterosaurs flourished more than 130 million years ago for about 80 million years. Their descendants became very large. The tail shortened and the teeth disappeared. A typical representative was the pteranodon, which lived during the Cretaceous period, about 144 to 66.4 million years ago. One fossil pteranodon had a wingspan of 27 feet (8 meters).

In 1971 the skeleton of the largest known flying animal, a pterosaur, was unearthed in Texas. Its wingspan was about 39 (12 meters). The pterosaurs, which became extinct along with the dinosaurs, are now believed not to have been direct ancestors of birds.

THE PTERODACTYL: FAST FACTS

1 A prehistoric flying reptile, the pterodactyl inhabited Europe and many other regions of the world.

2 It lived from the late Jurassic period through the late Cretaceous period, approximately 145 to 66 million years ago.

3 There were several different species of pterodactyls, some of which had incredible wingspans.

4 In general, pterodactyls had compact bodies, long necks, elongated skulls (which were crested in some species), and either greatly reduced or absent tails.

5 Pterodactyls were carnivorous. Several species that lived along the ocean coasts had teeth which were well adapted for feeding on fish. Pterodactyls that lived farther inland probably fed upon insects and small, land-dwelling animals.

EXTINCTION

The Cretaceous ended rather suddenly about 66 million years ago with a major extinction event that caused the end of the dinosaurs. This extinction is one of the worst known, with nearly 80 percent of all species destroyed.

WHAT WAS THE CAUSE?

The causes of the Cretaceous extinctions have been greatly debated. A huge volcanic outpouring at that time occurred in what is now India, forming the Deccan Traps (lava beds). Some scientists suggest that such activity would cause vast amounts of carbon dioxide and other gases to vent into the atmosphere, producing a massive greenhouse effect, with subsequent climate change and acid rain similar to that which occurred at the close of the Permian period. Other scientists have suggested that rearrangement of the Earth's landmasses through continental drift could have caused climate changes and disrupted habitats.

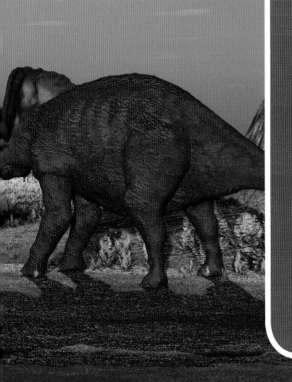

THE ASTEROID THEORY

The most widely accepted theory for what caused the Cretaceous extinctions, however, is the asteroid theory proposed by Walter Alvarez, a geologist, and his father Luis Alvarez, a physicist, in the 1980s. Walter Alvarez had discovered an excess concentration of the element iridium in the sediment layer deposited at the boundary between the Cretaceous and Tertiary periods, known as the K-T boundary. In about 1980 he and Luis Alvarez proposed an explanation. They said that, since iridium is common in meteorites, the layer could be explained as debris from the impact of a large body, perhaps 6 miles (10 kilometers) across. The devastation produced by such an impact could have easily caused mass extinctions.

WHERE WAS THE IMPACT?

By the mid-1990s other researchers had accumulated strong evidence that a major impact occurred about 65 million years ago in shallow seas at what is now the northern coast of Mexico's Yucatán Peninsula. Surveys of gravitational and magnetic fields in the region show a huge circular feature, now known as the Chicxulub crater, roughly 100 miles (160 kilometers) in diameter.

AN INCREDIBLE IMPACT

The environmental consequences of such an event would have been severe. The energy of the impact is estimated to have been about 100 million megatons—the equivalent of 2 million of the most powerful nuclear bombs ever detonated. Huge tsunamis, earthquakes, and intense heat would have been almost immediate effects. Within half an hour, material ejected from the site would have reentered the atmosphere over a large fraction of the globe. The shock-heating of the air would have set off huge forest fires. Longer-term effects would have included an almost complete cutoff of sunlight reaching the ground over much of the world, lasting for months. Chemicals produced by the event could have poisoned the air and oceans. Carbon dioxide released by the vaporization of seafloor sediment could have caused a large greenhouse effect lasting hundreds of years afterward.

FOSSILS

Fossils are the remains of ancient life that have been preserved in Earth's crust. Most people think of fossils as preserved bones or shells of primitive animals. However, there are many forms of fossils. Scientists have even found fossil impressions of early forms of bacteria.

Not all remains of living things become fossils. For fossilization to occur, an organism must be preserved soon after it dies or its tissues will quickly decay. Moist areas such as floodplains and riverbeds, where large amounts of sediment are deposited, are good settings for fossilization. The most common fossils come from hard tissues, such as shells, bones, and tree trunks. Soft tissues can fossilize if they are quickly preserved after the organism dies; this is relatively rare, however, since these tissues decay rapidly after death.

PRESERVING FOSSILS

Fossil collection as performed by scientists is difficult work that must be executed with great care. At a fossil site, scientists slowly and carefully remove specimens from rock using dental tools and similar instruments to avoid damaging the remains. As each part of the specimen is removed, it must be labeled and documented and its location within the rock noted. After careful analysis of the remains, most fossils are housed in museum and university collections.

FOR MORE INFORMATION,
SEE THE APP!

WHERE FOSSILS ARE FOUND

Some locations around the world are especially rich in fossils. Mongolia and China were sites of many key dinosaur finds in the late 20th and early 21st centuries. The Liaoning deposits in northeastern China have produced large numbers of feathered dinosaur fossils, thereby increasing the evidence for a close evolutionary relationship between dinosaurs and birds.

The largest and best-known deposits of fossilized dinosaur bones in the United States are at Dinosaur National Monument, a desert area in northwestern Colorado and northeastern Utah, that was set aside in 1915 to preserve the rich fossil beds it contained. The monument covers an area of 329 square miles (852 square kilometers). Excavations between 1909 and 1923 produced some 350 tons of dinosaur bones. Other U.S. sites abundant in dinosaur fossils include the tar pits of La Brea in California, Como Bluff and Lance Creek in Wyoming, and the Morrison and Canon City sites in Colorado.

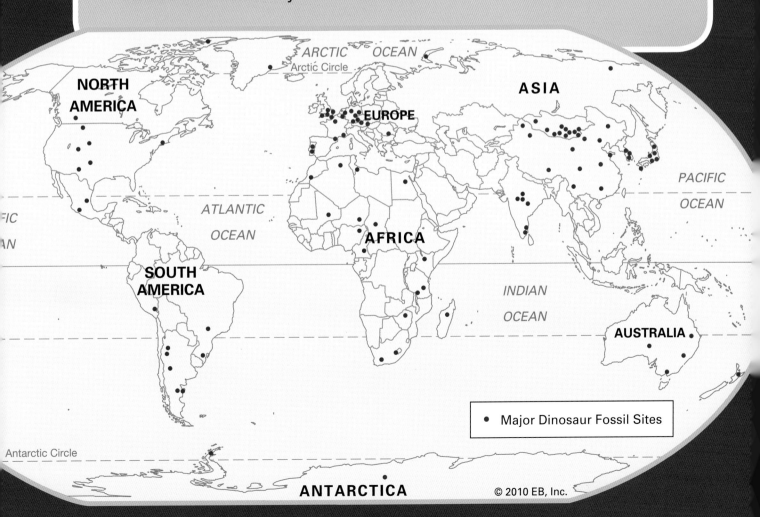

© 2010 EB, Inc.

FASCINATING FOSSIL FINDS

THE FIRST DINOSAUR FOSSILS

The first three dinosaurs ever to be described and named scientifically were found in England in the early 19th century. In 1824, William Buckland, a clergyman and amateur paleontologist, announced his discovery of the fossilized bones of *Megalosaurus*, a large theropod that lived during the mid-Jurassic period. The fossilized teeth and some bones of a duck-billed dinosaur from the Cretaceous period had been discovered somewhat earlier, but they were not formally described and named until 1825, when the discovery was announced by paleontologist Gideon Mantell. He named the new animal *Iguanodon*, because the fossil's teeth resembled those of an iguana.

In 1842, almost two decades after the first dinosaur discovery, the famous zoologist and anatomist Richard Owen coined the name dinosaur, meaning "terrible lizard," to encompass *Megalosaurus*, *Iguanodon*, and *Hylaeosaurus*, a Cretaceous ankylosaur discovered by Mantell and formally named in 1833.

Iguanodon.

A NEW TECHNOLOGY

A row of tail vertebrae was the first evidence of *Seismosaurus*, discovered in 1979 in the Ojito Wilderness Study Area located in New Mexico in the southwestern United States. Initial excavation of eight exposed tail vertebrae from a sandstone mesa in the Morrison Formation began in 1985 by paleontologist David D. Gillette, who formally named the dinosaur *Seismosaurus* in 1986. Excavating the remaining partial skeleton of this dinosaur was a challenge because it curved deeply into the mesa. Gillette was able to trace the remainder of the skeleton into the mesa by using seismic tomography—a method used to locate underground structures with sound waves. This was the first time such technology had been used to find dinosaur remains.

"GOOD MOTHER LIZARD"

The discovery of *Maiasaura* in 1978 was one of the most remarkable finds in the study of dinosaurs. Amid the fossils of a dinosaur nesting site in a mounded area in Montana, paleontologists found the remains of an adult *Maiasaura*, several presumed juveniles that measured about 3 feet (91 centimeters) in length, and several hatchlings that measured approximately 20 inches (51 centimeters). They also found numerous intact eggs and many broken shells, which scientists presume were trampled by hatchlings. The eggs appeared to have been laid with great care, arranged in circles, and layered with earth or sand in a manner that would have helped incubate the eggs as well as shield them from predators.

The evidence from the Montana site indicates that *Maiasaura* was a social animal, with mothers laying eggs and caring for their young in large dinosaur nurseries. This behavior gives this dinosaur its name: *Maiasaura* means "good mother lizard."

A CHANGING FIELD

Sometimes, scientists change their theories about dinosaurs over time or in response to new evidence.

NOT A THIEF

The first fossil evidence of *Oviraptor*—collected in 1923 at a site in Omnogov in southern Mongolia—inspired its name, which means "egg thief." The bones were found atop a clutch of what were thought to be *Protoceratops* eggs, leading paleontologists to presume that *Oviraptor* had been in the act of stealing the eggs for food. Fossils discovered in the 1990s, however, showed *Oviraptor* apparently crouched over clutches of eggs, suggesting that it was trying to protect the nests, which likely contained its own eggs, rather than plunder them. Scientists now believe that *Oviraptor* may have fed mainly on mollusks, using its beak to crush the shells.

Oviraptor.

SAFER ON THE GROUND

The first fossil evidence of *Hypsilophodon* was discovered on the Isle of Wight in the mid–19th century. Because of a series of misinterpretations of the evidence, *Hypsilophodon* was initially thought to be a tree dweller. A reassessment of the evidence in 1974, however, led paleontologists to conclude that *Hypsilophodon* lived on the ground.

JUST ONE DINOSAUR

The first fossil evidence of *Psittacosaurus* was found in Mongolia in 1922 and described by paleontologist Henry Fairfield Osborn in 1923. Although Osborn described two different genera from the remains, *Psittacosaurus* and *Protiguanidon*, further examination revealed that the two dinosaurs were synonymous and led scientists to drop the name *Protiguanidon*.

The smallest dinosaur yet discovered was a *Psittacosaurus* juvenile that measured just over 9 inches (23 centimeters) long.

Fossils of dinosaur eggs.

STILL A MYSTERY

The unique dinosaur *Segnosaurus* has long mystified paleontologists. Although it has several physical features typical of the bird-hipped dinosaur order Ornithischia, *Segnosaurus* is classified in the lizard-hipped order Saurischia. Some paleontologists further argue that *Segnosaurus* belongs to the Theropoda, a group that includes carnivorous, or flesh-eating, dinosaurs such as *Allosaurus*. Others agree that it is more closely related to the sauropodomorphs, ancestors of the giant herbivorous sauropods, such as *Brachiosaurus*.

As more fossils from *Segnosaurus* are found, scientists will be better able to solve the classification mystery of this unusual dinosaur.

Segnosaurus.

PALEONTOLOGY

Paleontology is the study of prehistoric life that involves the analysis of plant and animal fossils—including those of microscopic size—preserved in rocks. This discipline is concerned with all aspects of the biology of ancient life-forms, including shape and structure, evolutionary patterns, taxonomic relationships with each other and with modern living species, geographic distribution, and interrelationships with the environment.

The field of paleontology dates back to the early 1800s. In 1815 the English geologist William Smith demonstrated the value of using fossils for the study of rock formations. About the same time, the French zoologist Georges Cuvier initiated studies comparing the structure of living animals with fossil remains.

FIVE NAMES TO KNOW

Mary Anning (1799–1847). Prolific English fossil hunter and amateur anatomist Mary Anning is credited with the discovery of several dinosaur specimens that assisted in the early development of paleontology. In 1810 her brother found the first known *Ichthyosaurus* specimen; however, she was the one who excavated it. Her most famous find occurred in 1824 when she uncovered the first intact *Plesiosaurus* skeleton.

Mary Anning's family relied on the sale of fossils collected from seaside cliffs near their home along England's Channel coast as a source of income.

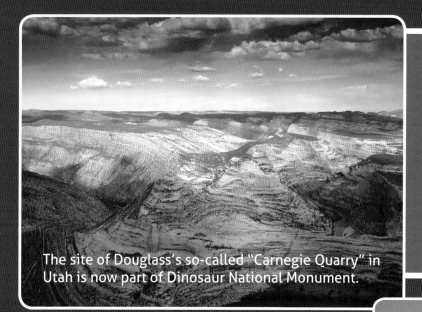

The site of Douglass's so-called "Carnegie Quarry" in Utah is now part of Dinosaur National Monument.

Earl Douglass (1862–1931). Between 1909 and 1923, Earl Douglass sent the Carnegie Museum more than 300 tons of excavated remains of dinosaurs and other animals of the Jurassic Period. Workers at his dig uncovered 20 complete or nearly complete skeletons, including a *Diplodocus* nearly 100 feet (30 meters) long.

The state of New Mexico adopted the *Coelophysis* as its state fossil.

Edwin Colbert (1905–2001). U.S. vertebrate paleontologist Edwin Colbert shaped the study of dinosaurs and evolution in the middle decades of the 20th century. He found thousands of fossils, discovering at least 50 new species. His first great dinosaur fossil discovery came in 1947, when he found a group of complete *Coelophysis* skeletons at Ghost Ranch in north central New Mexico. Colbert's find showed that the early 6-foot- (1.8-meter-) long dinosaur had traveled in herds and had taken some care of its young.

John Ostrom (born 1928). The idea that birds evolved from dinosaurs, first proposed by Thomas Henry Huxley in the 1860s, had few supporters before John Ostrom demonstrated a century later that some dinosaurs are more like ostriches than lizards.

In 1964, Ostrom found a previously unknown dinosaur with clawed hands and the teeth of a meat-eater, *Deinonychus*.

Robert Bakker (born 1945). Robert Bakker did much to revitalize popular interest in dinosaurs in the 1970s. Disdaining the conventional theories, Bakker said that dinosaurs were fast, smart, sophisticated, social, agile, erect, and warm-blooded. While scientists debated particulars, popular culture absorbed Bakker's new vision of dinosaurs, as depicted in the 1993 film *Jurassic Park*.

TEST WHAT YOU KNOW

1. All theropods were meat eaters.
   True   False

2. Modern birds arose from the subgroup Ornithopoda.
   True   False

3. Which dinosaur was longer?
   Apatosaurus   *Seismosaurus*

4. *Tyrannosaurus rex* was a carnosaur.
   True   False

5. Which dinosaur weighed more?
   Tyrannosaurus rex   *Allosaurus*

6. Dinosaurs in the family Dromaeosauridae were known for this characteristic.
   A sickle-shaped claw   Three horns
   A neck frill

7. *Iguanodon* was the first dinosaur discovered.
   True   False

8. *Maiasaura* was a crested hadrosaur.
   True   False

9. All members of the ceratopsid family had horns.
   True   False

10. Which dinosaur was larger?
    Triceratops   *Stegosaurus*

6 MONTHS FREE

ENCYCLOPÆDIA
Britannica ONLINE©

This certificate entitles you to use
Encyclopædia Britannica Online© **FREE FOR 6 MONTHS!**

Your subscription will begin on the day you activate your account by following these simple instructions:

1. Access the online registration form provided at: **www.britannica.com/certificate**
2. Enter the Promotion Code that appears below.
3. Follow the steps to create your password and account profile.

Promotion Code: **EBVR2017** Codes must be redeemed by:
December 31, 2021

TROUBLESHOOTING

The image I see is blurry.

Make sure the smartphone is aligned precisely with the center of the viewer.
Adjusting the phone left or right a few millimeters can make a big difference.
The tilt of the viewer and the phone can also affect how the screen looks to you.
You can also try to calibrate the viewer using one of the QR codes found below.

I was asked to allow the app to take pictures.
Do I need to allow this?

Yes, this allows the app to take a picture of the QR code in your book in
order to validate your purchase and access the accompanying app.

How do I calibrate my viewer?

If asked to calibrate your viewer, scan the first of the QR codes found below. If the picture seems
blurry afterward, touch the small gear icon that appears at one corner of your screen. You will
then be given an opportunity to Switch Viewers. Scan the other QR code found here. Some
smartphones work better with one calibration, while others work better with the second.

I'm getting a pop-up that this app won't work without Google VR Services, asking me to install it before continuing. Do I need to do this?

Click Cancel; it should not prevent you from running the app successfully.

Can I use this viewer with other apps?

The viewer is a standard size that is designed to be compatible with many apps. Try it out!

I damaged my viewer. Can I use this app with other viewers?

Yes, this app is compatible with many other standard-sized viewers on the market.

My screen gets dim when I place it in the viewer.

Check your phone settings. Under Display settings, if there is a setting such as "Auto adjust
brightness," where the screen adapts to lighting conditions, turn that setting off.